WITHDRAWN

FRENCH GENERAL

TREASURED NOTIONS

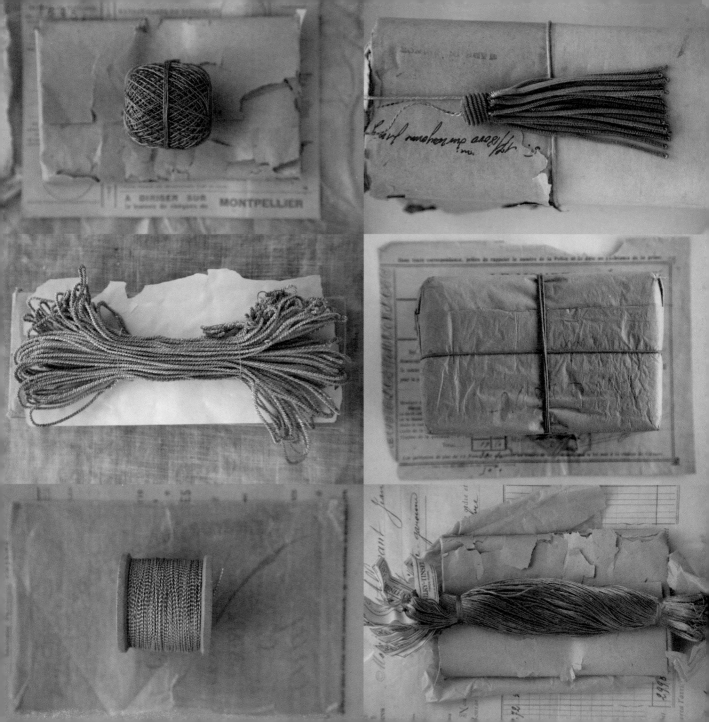

FRENCH GENERAL

TREASURED NOTIONS

Inspiration and Craft Projects Using Vintage Beads, Buttons, Ribbons, and Trim from Tinsel Trading Company

· · · · · · · · · · · · · · · ·

By KAARI MENG

Photographs by JON ZABALA   *Foreword by* MARCIA CEPPOS

CHRONICLE BOOKS
SAN FRANCISCO

Library of Congress Cataloging-in-Publication Data:

Meng, Kaari.
    French General : treasured notions : inspiration
and craft projects using vintage beads, buttons,
ribbons, and trim from Tinsel Trading Company /
by Kaari Meng ; foreword by Marcia Ceppos ; photographs by Jon Zabala.
        p. cm.
    Includes index.
    ISBN-13: 978-0-8118-6890-7
    ISBN-10: 0-8118-6890-7
    1. Handicraft. 2. Handicraft—Equipment and
supplies. I. Title.

    TT857.M46 2010
    745.5—dc22

            2009019271

Manufactured in China
Designed by Katie Heit

Bakelite is a registered trademark of Union Cambridge
Corp. Dremel is a registered trademark of the Robert
Bosch Tool Corporation. Mod Podge is a registered
trademark of the Enterprise Paint Manufacturing
Co. Styrofoam is a registered trademark of the Dow
Chemical Company. X-ACTO is a registered trademark
of Elmer's Products, Inc.

10 9 8 7 6 5 4 3 2 1

Chronicle Books LLC
680 Second Street
San Francisco, CA 94107
www.chroniclebooks.com

CONTENTS

❧ FOREWORD ❧

Time stopped in 1940 in Tinsel Trading's basement: the walls' peeling paint, the old rusted shelves, the acidic smell of metal, and endless boxes overflowing with vintage thread, tassels, trims, and fringes—a collection of goods that spans seventy-five years and was hidden until now. This remarkable treasure trove is the product of one man's—my grandfather's—obsession with unique notions. It started with a casual interest in shiny gold-and-silver threads and grew into the most extraordinary inventory of materials gathered from all over the world. To this day, a large amount of this inventory remains in our basement, still wound on the French manufacturers' original wooden spools and wrapped in paper with handwritten gold labels. Many notions still nest safely in the handmade wooden crates sent by sea from France. I hope to keep these authentic crates closed for as long as possible, perpetuating the history and mystery of my grandfather's company, Tinsel Trading Company.

After a brief job as a mechanic for the army during WWI, my grandfather, Arch Bergoffen, went to work in Manhattan at the French Tinsel Co., a vendor of metal threads made in France. Because his father was a tailor, Arch was intrigued by the threads and spent years working for the company. Eventually, in 1933,

he purchased the business and began his own: Tinsel Trading Company was born.

During World War II, his biggest client turned out to be the U.S. government. Unable to import metal threads for sewing and embroidering military uniforms, the government relied on my grandfather, who had stockpiled thousands and thousands of spools of metal thread. With European fashion at a wartime standstill, American designers began to emerge as industry trendsetters. Metal thread was in demand and Tinsel Trading was the only place to go.

After the war, my grandfather realized he needed to offer a wider variety of embellishments. Tinsel Trading would always specialize in metals, but he grew the business to include trims, tassels, fringes, cords, fabrics, and all sorts of wonders. He hunted for anything made before 1950. Soon, word got out to every vendor and salesman and he never had to travel further than the front door. Everyone who had "old" and "useless" stuff lying around—most of it from outside the United States—had heard about that crazy guy on 38th Street who would buy almost any kind of trim as long as it was old. Little did they know that their junk was gold to my grandfather. He bought beautiful *ombre* ribbons woven in France, glass buttons made in Czechoslovakia, French and German tassels, raffia ornaments produced in Italy, and anything else that attracted him (even

Brazilian beetles from the 1930s). If it remotely fit into his idea of a creative decorative item, he wanted it.

Hundreds of boxes arrived over the years—many went unopened. One piece of each item would be put out for sale on the shelves, but the rest went down into the basement, one box piled on top of another, blocking aisles and passageways, sitting unopened and unmarked. Eventually those years turned into decades and when my grandfather died in 1989, the basement was filled with thousands and thousands of items. It was an unorganized, cluttered mass of wonderment. All you could do was gaze in astonishment.

Now, for the first time, I'm thrilled to share these wonders with the world. After my grandfather passed away, it became my job to bring Tinsel Trading into the next century. It would be a formidable and at times overwhelming task, but I knew I could and would accomplish it. My passion and determination would carry me through. Along the way, the people I have met during this adventure have been most remarkable: famous movie stars, singers, architects, and fashion designers such as Ralph Lauren, Anna Sui, and John Galliano. Every day I meet amazing artists and talented everyday crafters who just want to create something special.

I met Kaari Meng in the early 1990s when she was designing wholesale costume jewelry. We immediately recognized that we shared a love for antique notions. Over the years we became friends. For years, "When can I see the basement?" was Kaari's mantra whenever we spoke. I would laugh and repeat my own mantra, "No one goes to the basement except my employees." There were times I thought she would apply for a job just to get a chance to see what lay below.

I finally relented to Kaari's pleading. Was that ever the right move! In May 2008, Kaari and her sister, Molly, came to New York. With barely contained excitement, they headed down the narrow steps to what Kaari had waited for, for over fifteen years. That day, they spent hours exploring the basement. Every few minutes I would check to see if they were still breathing. Oohs, aahs, and gasps confirmed that they were never better.

This book shares Kaari's experience that day and our belief that with beautiful ingredients, anything is possible. I hope you enjoy the tour.

—Marcia Ceppos
Owner, Tinsel Trading Company

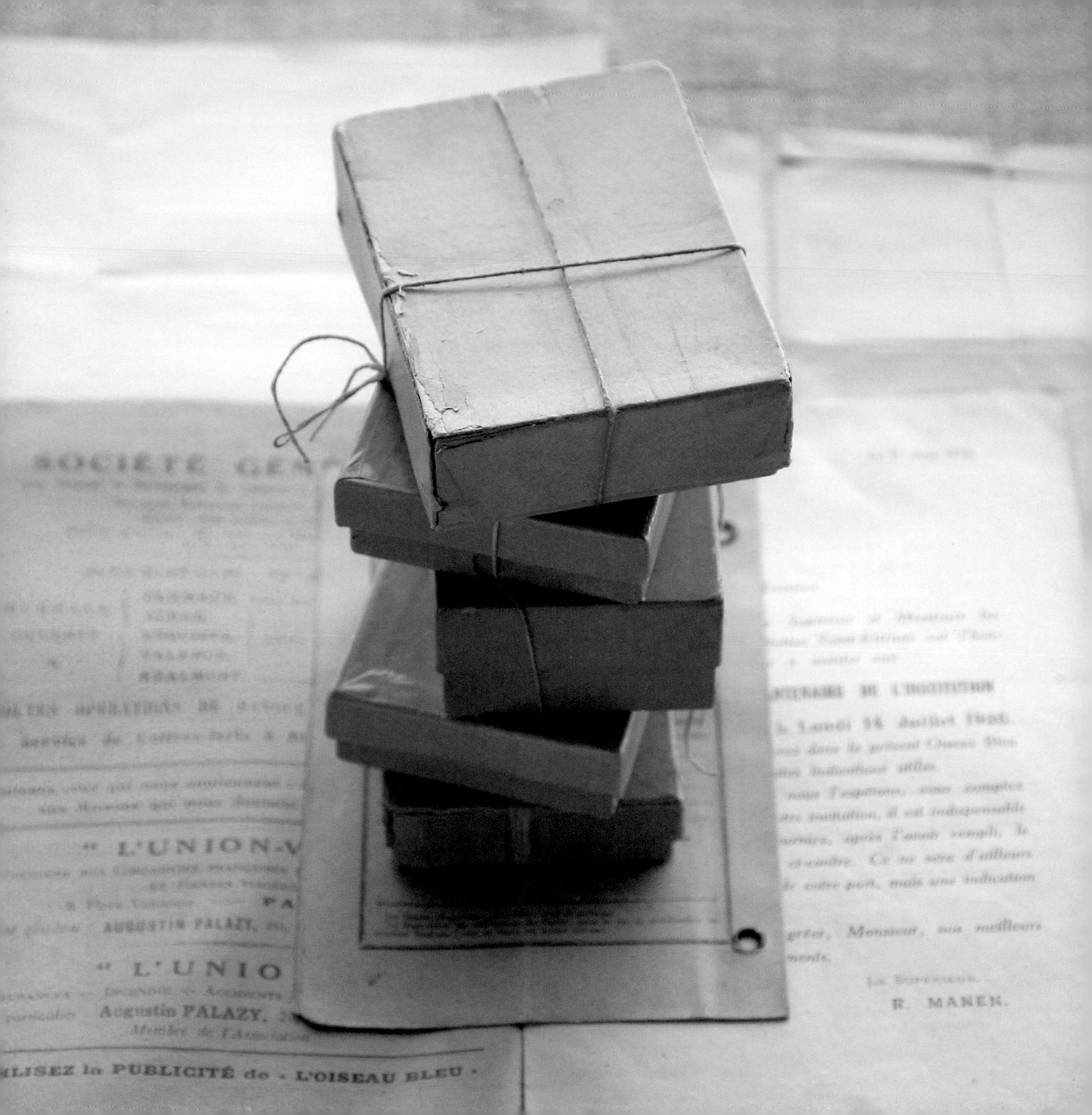

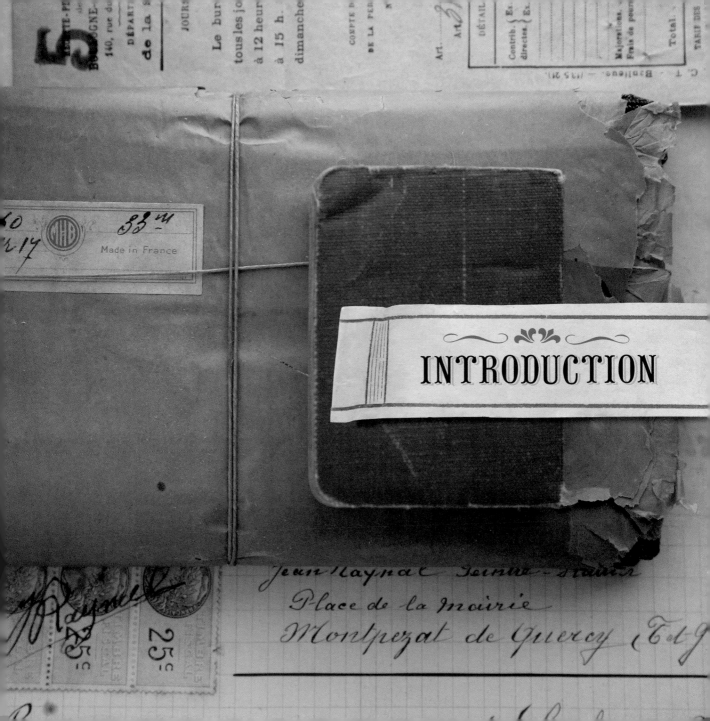

INTRODUCTION

Jean Raynal Peintre-Statuur
Place de la mairie
Montpezat de Quercy (T et G)

When I started my jewelry business, Kaari Meng Designs, back in 1992, I rented a small studio on the second floor of an old building on 38th Street in New York City. I created a line of costume jewelry based on vintage beads, buttons, and baubles. Since that time, I have been obsessed with finding vintage notions to use in jewelry making and other craft projects. I look for everything from milk glass stamens to coral velvet leaves. I used to search out treasures in the millinery and trim district of Manhattan—an area with dozens of old shops selling ribbons, flowers, feathers, beads, buttons, and trim to fashion designers. I would spend my lunch hour walking up and down the blocks between 5th and 6th Avenues looking for stores or private stashes of old notions. Once I found a shop carrying great old stock, I always asked if I could visit their basement. Usually, I was warned the basements were dark, cramped, and unorganized. Even better, I would think. In the basement, I would set to work digging out the gems that were hidden underneath decades of inventory. I was looking for batches of the odd and unusual bits left behind—materials so popular in their day, thousands and thousands of pieces were made to accommodate the ladies' decorative-trim business.

On one of my many hunting and gathering trips in the neighborhood, I happened upon Tinsel Trading Company, an old trim shop that sold metallic ribbons, appliqués, tassels, and all sorts of decorative embellishments. The walls were stacked as high as the ceiling with old cardboard boxes, each one filled with a collection from the past. The very first item I bought at Tinsel Trading was a spool of 30 yards of French metallic *ombre* ribbon.

I used this ribbon in a line of jewelry I designed for Anthropologie. I linked together a strand of old glass pearls and tied the ribbon in the back instead of using a clasp. When I finished using the spool I went back to Tinsel Trading to dig for another roll or two. On this second visit, I met Marcia Ceppos, the store's owner.

Marcia assured me that she had hundreds of rolls of my particular *ombre* ribbon—in fact, a whole basement full. But she insisted it was too unorganized to understand; only she knew where everything was. Marcia wasn't interested in explaining her organized chaos to anybody,

especially not a stranger. For fifteen years I attempted to get down into Marcia's basement. I just had to see for myself the treasures that had been hidden away for so many years. Each time I asked Marcia if I could take a peek, just glimpse at the stock, the answer was always no. "No" kept me going back to Tinsel Trading for years.

In 1999, I opened French General in Soho, and began to put to use all of the notions I had been collecting for so many years. I quickly learned that there were many uses for them beyond jewelry making, such as propping displays and creating inspiration boards. I discovered that there were others who were also interested in these forgotten decorative bits that were so highly cherished in the 19th and early-20th centuries. All of the beads, *cabachons*, sequins, and feathers that I had dug out of basements were put on display in large, old apothecary jars. The color, texture, and age of these notions resonated with other crafters and collectors and we soon had a loyal following. Our stock included hand-curled feathers, Venetian glass fruit beads,

and velvet millinery flowers—all antique notions that could be used for inspiration and crafting.

Marcia and I continued our friendship and knew we would eventually work together. When I heard Tinsel Trading was moving out of its building after seventy years, I knew it was time to (finally) get down into the basement and dig out some gold. Before Marcia packed up every box, my sister, Molly, and I donned masks and gloves and spent hours upon hours pulling out one of each and every notion specimen from the old boxes.

What we found in Marcia's basement was beauty to our eyes. Through the layers of old boxes and tissue paper, we found envelopes that had been carefully hand wrapped and filled with silver metal sequins, handmade sequin appliqués, and linen-wrapped buttons. Labeled on the outside with small writing in French that simply said, *Fabrique en France, un grosse*. Many of the boxes had never been opened and the goods were waiting untouched to be explored and brought to good use. Molly

and I would pull out each and every notion, examine it, and then place it in our pack box. When we finally finished, we were covered in layers of old dust and dirt—but we couldn't have been happier.

In this special book, you will see what my sister and I uncovered: a curated collection of materials that have been around for over a hundred years and are as contemporary and classic as anything made today. Alongside the materials, I share an idea or two on how to craft and work with these old materials or how to find similar material to work with. Although Tinsel has packed up and moved around the corner off Fifth Avenue, you can still find some of these very same notions in their emporium of embellishments—or look for similar material in your favorite basements. Who knows, the perfect notions might even be in your craft box already.

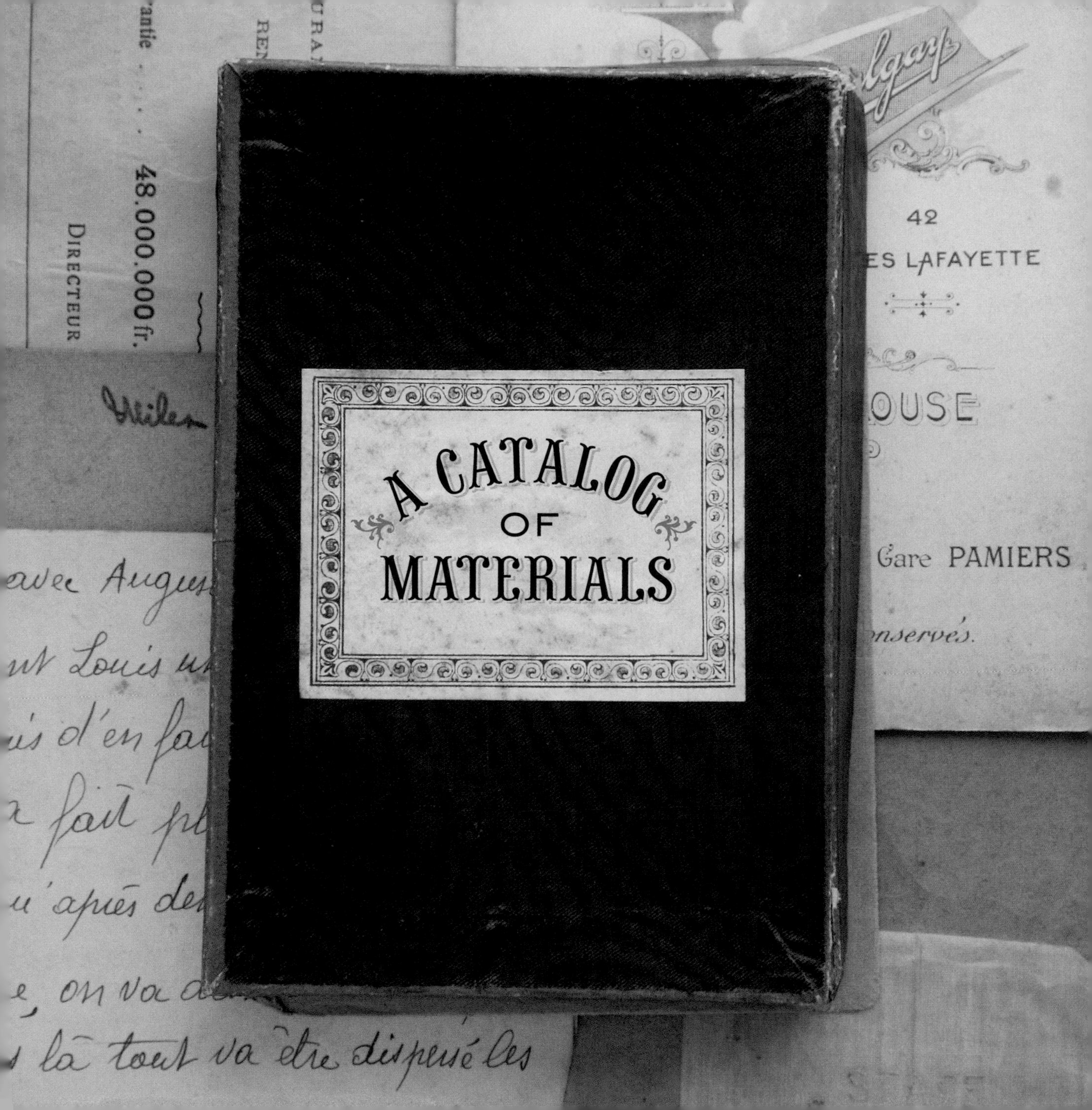
A CATALOG
OF
MATERIALS

MILITARY RIBBON *(opposite page)*
This heavy, metallic, striped ribbon was made in France throughout the 19th and 20th centuries for French military uniforms and flags.

BULLION *(above)*
Bullion is made from a metal wire wound into a hollow tubular shape. During the 1930s, bullion was typically made in Europe and Tinsel Trading was the only company producing it in America. Bullion comes in a wide range of colors today and is commonly used for embroidery on fabric and for military uniforms.

COILED WIRE *(below)*
This coiled wire was made in the Tinsel Trading basement with a tool that crimps and coils the wire as it passes through a machine. It makes a great bead for jewelry or crafts when cut into small strips.

BUTTONS *(left)*

All sorts of materials were used to make buttons in the 19th century: mother-of-pearl, glass, metal, and Bakelite were just a few. Buttons were a small, inexpensive notion that could instantly add charm to a simple jacket or dress. Collected, hoarded, and stashed, buttons continue to be a favorite material to craft and make jewelry with.

METALLIC RIBBON *(opposite page)*

Ribbon made with metal thread became popular during the early 1920s and 1930s when it was commonly used for *passementerie*—elaborate trimmings for clothes and furniture.

GOLD TASSELS *(below)*

Old gold bullion tassels made out of coiled wire and a wooden bead at top were used in banners and military epaulets. Tassels this small can be used to make simple drops on jewelry or small bags.

GOLD FRINGE *(above right)*

Old gold fringe is made of metal thread and was used for special award ribbons and banners. Lightly tacked together with string, the fringe is snipped loose once sewn onto a project.

METAL THREAD *(opposite page)*

Metal thread was used in many decorative crafts and clothing embellishments during the 19th and 20th centuries. Shiny, matte, corrugated, or flattened, each one went through a separate process to achieve its unique texture and style.

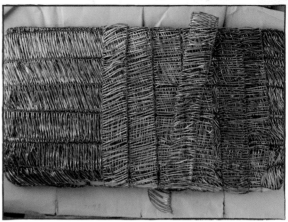

BEETLES *(above)*

For centuries, dried beetles have been a truly unique notion for jewelry making. Furniture designers, artists, museum curators, and many others have also sought out these specimens. The green-iris color on the beetles' underbellies proves that all of our wildest color inspiration comes directly from nature.

METALLIC TRIM *(above)*

Delicate metallic trim hand-assembled in France was made for embellishing clothing. Trim this soft and light is perfect for hat trim.

MOTHER-OF-PEARL BUTTONS

(opposite page)

These carved mother-of-pearl buttons were hand-stitched onto a metallic button card. The nacre in the button was thought to reflect one's spirit.

METAL CABACHONS *(below)*

These fine metal *cabachons* were stamped out of very soft metal sheets for embellishing jewelry. Because of the metal's softness, these *cabachons* can be stitched down to paper or fabric.

DARK GOLD RIBBON *(above)*

Originally used for military costumes, this old gold ribbon is wonderful for ribbon work or millinery flowers.

MILLINERY LEAVES *(opposite page)*

Small, delicate, hand-pressed leaves and petals were used to construct millinery flowers or corsages. These leaves were also used for decorating wedding cakes.

GOLD CORD *(below)*
Metal thread and cotton cord that has a wider center every other inch was often used to do stump work and other hand-stitching crafts.

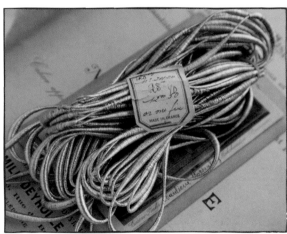

METAL FLORAL RIBBON *(above)*
Early woven metallic ribbon with botanical prints was very popular during the 1920s and 1930s. Used for embellishing home interiors as well as clothing, this trim is beautiful on both of its sides.

BAUBLE TASSELS *(opposite page)*
These tassels were handmade by wrapping antique metal thread around a wooden base. They are remarkable examples of what can be accomplished with thread and an imagination.

OMBRE RIBBON *(opposite page)*

Multihued ribbon like this is called *ombre*, "shadow," because of the shadows, or gradation, of color. This vintage sample, in dusty shades of rose, was one of hundreds Tinsel Trading imported from France during the 20th century. Many *ombre* ribbons have wire in the edges, which makes them ideal materials for crafting beautiful ribbon flowers.

SAMPLE CARDS *(above)*

Tailors and craftsmen relied on beautiful handmade sample cards to re-order their materials. This one dates back to the early 1900s, and is filled with small swatches of metallic trims and fringes.

SEQUINS *(above)*

Known as *spangles* or *pailletes* in French, these sequins were fabricated in France in the 1890s from copper metal, then silver plated. Sequins are now made in all different shapes and sizes and have a variety of textures.

GROSGRAIN RIBBON *(left)*

Striped or dotted ribbon was a favorite millinery material when men and women wore hats every Sunday and they wanted to be able to change their hat bands to match their outfits.

GLASS BEADS *(above)*

Although not technically thread, this spool of glass beads would give the impression of a beaded cord when stitched down to fabric. It is a lovely example of early French trim used primarily for military décor.

METAL COLORED WIRE *(page 37)*

Plating copper metal before it's spun into wire creates the different colors of these wires. A collection of deep shades of teal and olivine green makes a natural palette.

GLASS BEADS *(above)*

Bugle and seed beads were made all over Europe to supply beaders with the most unusual color combinations. The more cuts a bead has, the more shine the glass gives off.

SPOOLED WIRE *(above)*

Old silver and gold spools of wire could be used for tatting or fine embroidery on religious garments.

METALLIC FABRIC *(opposite page)*

Elegant attire was fashioned out of material woven together with metallic threads. Decorative trims and fabrics were also manufactured for elaborate wedding veils and dresses.

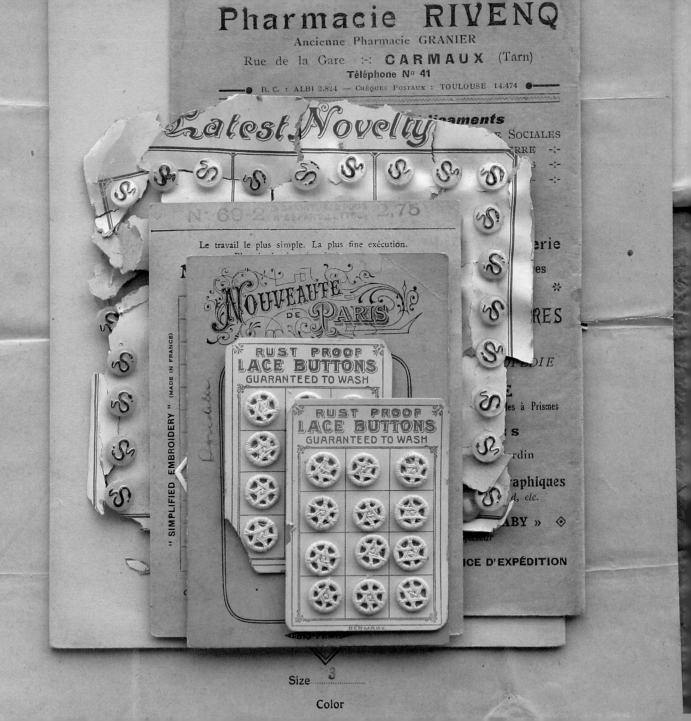

HUNTING AND GATHERING NOTIONS

N° 1832

F M

AFDR

Monsieur

204

que d'après votre ordre et pour

novembre

Vendu

votre

13.

Courtage et

Ensemble

N.-B. Un avis ultérieur annoncera l'arrivée

Veuillez agréer, Monsieur

Rapporter le pr

Toujours la même vie, qu'il
bien a y mettre fin, car le jour
qui sera certes té bien venu. Aey
nous avons la pluie, qui rafraîchi
la température qui commençait
un peu chaude. On ne s'en
du tout je vous assure, mais

I look for old notions everywhere I go—antique shops, fabric shops, estate sales, flea markets, and, when I am lucky, an old basement! Usually, people who trade in the vintage textile business come upon trunks full of old crafting materials. Finding gold usually happens when digging through baskets of old supplies. You may not see exactly what you were looking for on top of the pile, but look a little deeper and you may find the special notion you need. Los Angeles and New York both have large textile trading districts. Walking these neighborhoods and peeking into doors usually leads to an interesting collection of goods. For more ideas on where to hunt out your own treasures, see the Resources section. Remember to follow a thread—one old collection of notions might lead you to another.

Always test the age of the material before you buy it. If you are planning on crafting with old materials, as opposed to just displaying them for inspiration, you will want to know if the thread can withstand the demands of your project. Pull slightly on the thread, ribbon, or fabric to get a good sense of the fragility of the material. If you can pull it apart easily, it's probably best not to use it for anything other than a decorative item on an inspiration board. Don't shy away from dust or grime.

Beads, as long as they are not chipped, can be caked with dirt and will come out sparkling if you clean them properly. Most glass beads can be washed in warm, sudsy water and then strained to dry. Plastic and celluloid sequins or beads should be dusted off with a cloth, as they can soften or melt when exposed to water.

Old wood and metal notions should also be dusted off, to retain the natural luster and not damage the patina. When in doubt, ask the vendors. They likely have some tricks of their own to share.

When you can, buy in bulk—even if it means buying more than you need for your project. Good old unused stock won't be around forever. I will scoop up a case of chenille snails without hesitation because I know I will never see a full box of such a rare find ever again. I will come up with a use for them eventually! Buy what you can afford and know you will put it all to good use, even if it's for tying onto small gifts for friends or pinning to your inspiration board.

Store all of your vintage notions in a cool, dry place away from any moisture or heat. Laying them out flat in shoeboxes or stashing them in glass jars is a way to keep them safe and accessible when you are ready to use them. A shoe bag hanging on the back of a door is another great way to organize your collection. I like to store all of my notions by color so when I am working on a dusty teal bracelet, I know I can find inspiration in my blue box.

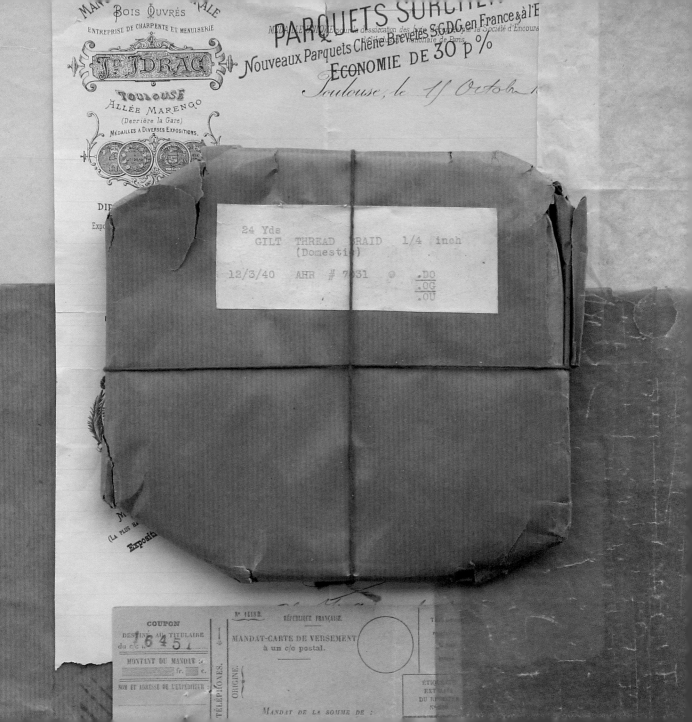

GRENOBLE - CASERNE - DODE

Grenoble 18 Juin 1933

Chers parents

David A Murray.

READING CLUES
FROM
THE PAST

Nº 1418 B.

RÉPUBLIQUE F

MANDAT-CARTE DE VERSEM
à un c/c postal.

la taxe

perçue.

ÉTIQUETTE
EXTRAITE
DU REGISTRE
Nº 510.

MANDAT DE LA SOMME DE :
(Montant de la somme, francs en lettres)

CADRE A REMPLIR
par le bureau d'émission

Somme en chiffres

fr.

A inscrire au compte courant
désigné ci-dessous :

Numéro et date d'émission (1).

MONTPELLIER C.C 764 5 F
MAISON TOURRETTE-F11ERE

This imported article of synthetic phenolic resin was manufactured by a foreign concern in no wise connected with the Bakelite Corp. and American corpor.
MADE IN CZECHOSLOVAKIA

This imported article of synthetic phenolic resin was manufactured by a foreign concern in no wise connected with the Bakelite Corp. and American corpor.
MADE IN CZECHOSLOVAKIA

The packaging on a wrapped notion or spool of trim can tell you so much information about the notion's age, source, and even what it might have been used for originally. The carefully wrapped boxes, the old tissue paper, the handwritten tags—all of these little details give us clues about where the notion is from and when it was made. Whenever I find old pieces that are still in their original packaging, I leave the pieces in the packaging and then write out the details that I can observe:

* How old does the box look? Is it made by hand, lined with paper?
* Is the writing on the packaging stamped, typed, or handwritten?
* Are there any names of a manufacturer, shipper, or vendor?
* Is the material packaged by the dozen or the gross (144 pieces)?

After pondering these questions, I look at the notion itself and try to determine if it was made by hand or machine. Did someone sit and hand sew all of the ends of the ribbon together, or were they machine sewn?

Typically, many of the notions out of Europe during the 19th and early 20th centuries were all hand wrapped, sewn, and packaged, so seeing these clues would lead me to believe the notion could be from the turn of the 20th century (plus or minus a few years).

Sometimes, if I am lucky, there might be a small sample of what the notion was used for, such as beads sewn onto a cloth or thread braided into a band. These small samples make up part of the history giving the notion actual life—somebody actually did sit and craft with this copper thread or wire-embedded bead.

I tend to save the old packaging even after using all of the notions inside. The patina, texture, and fragility of old packaging material cannot be reproduced. The one-inch brown paper that lined a spool of ribbon or the soft cotton batting that protected the crystal *cabachons*—these simple, organic colors work so well next to the colorful embellishments.

Poids déclaré

Dans toute corresponda... ...la date de l'échéance de la prime.

LE MONDE

Compagnie d'Assurances à Primes fixes contre l'Incendie, la Foudre, et les Explosions de toute nature

AUTORISÉE PAR DÉCRET DU 27 AVRIL 1864

Transformée en Société anonyme libre par délibération des Assemblées générales
des 2 Décembre 1879 et 15 Mai 1880.

2e Trimestre 1906

AGENCE GÉNÉRALE

79786

Série Q

POLICE

1362

Reçu de M

demeurant à Mo...

la somme de

pour la prime échue de

1907

1906

MATCHING
YESTERDAY'S COLORS

DÉCOMPTE

Montant de la prime.

Perçu pour le Tr...

Loi des 23 Août 1871 et 31 Décem...

Loi de finances du 13 Avril 18...

Droits de timbre, 0 fr. 04 o/oo.........

Coût de la Police ...... 2 fr. »

Timbre de la quittance. » 10

général,

GNIE :

10c.
QUITTANCES

Mart...

Gén...

TOTAL....... 17 6

Les quittances de plus de 10 francs sont assujetties au timbre de ...entimes, que la loi met à la charge de l'Assuré.

REMITTER SHOULD WRITE HERE NAME AND ADDRESS OF PERSON TO WHOM THE

...R WAS SENT:

TO

...RESS:

When digging for old notions, keep your eye out for colors that might have been in fashion during our great-grandmothers' time—the colors of the 1920s and 1930s were quite different from what we see in jewelry or fabric today. The soft grays and pinks with metallic silver threads or the Capri blues and teals woven together to look like the sea— all evoke an earlier place and time. Experiment with the old golds and mother-of-pearl—pairing colors that will add elegance to your projects or collage boards.

Ecole Saint-Théodard de Montauban

IMMUNITAS Communicetur

SCIENTIÆ ET VIRTUTI.

Toulouse, le 1 Octobre 1892

TOULOUSE
ALLÉE MARENGO
(Derrière la Gare)
MÉDAILLES A DIVERSES EXPOSITIONS.

DIPLÔME D'HONNEUR
Exposition Internationale de Toulouse, 1887

Marque de Fabrique Déposée
ENTREPÔTS
DANS LES PRINCIPALES VILLES
DU MIDI.

MÉDAILLE DE 1re CLASSE
(LA PLUS HAUTE RÉCOMPENSE DÉCERNÉE AU GROUPE DU BOIS)
Exposition des ARTS DÉCORATIFS
PARIS, 1884

VERRES DU NORD
ET DU MIDI
FABRIQUE DE VERNIS
a l'alcool
VERNIS GRAS
Huiles cuites, Siccatifs
Brillant universel
pour meubles et parquets

COULEURS, VERNIS
VERRES A VITRES
VERNIS FRANÇAIS & ANGLAIS
(USINE A MONROSE)

HENRI BOYER
vard St-Cyr et rue Calmel, 3 et 5
EUVE-SUR-LOT
-ET-GARONNE)

M

INSPIRATION
BOARDS

Allemant

Place de la Mairie à S

meilleurs salutations,

When I experiment with a new color palette, I start with a 8-by-8-in/20-by-20-cm hemp-covered inspiration board. I use the natural hemp as a base to ground the brighter, more vibrant colors from the notions. I then layer different scraps of fabric or notions together until I find a color combination that is based on old objects but has a freshness that will still be current. I add in small bits of inspiration in the same color family—anything that has the perfect shade of old pink will do, even if it's an old tag or label off a box. I gather color inspiration from everywhere. Beads, buttons, beetles— whatever inspires you at the moment should make it onto the board. Once I finish a color board, I hang it in my workshop for inspiration. I may end up using the palette for a jewelry line or to design a new line of fabric. Or, I may just use it for a place to rest my eyes when my head is swirling with ideas.

I look back over the years at all of the color boards I have made up and can see where each one has taken me in a different design direction—they serve as a small history of my collection of notions.

I hope this book inspires you to begin working with vintage materials, if you haven't already found out how special they are. Treasured notions, such as those Molly and I found in Marcia's basement, are a rare look into the past. These small tokens taken from a decorative life will amaze you with their beauty and charm.

QUITTANCE DE PRIME
LIBRAIRIE-IMPRIMERIE-PAPETERIE
es de Classes et de Bureaux
Madame Passama
Place Nationale
BEAUMONT-DE-LOMAGNE
4 FEUILLES
4 ENVELOPPES
HOTEL
MARY
ÉCOUCHÉ
David A Murray.

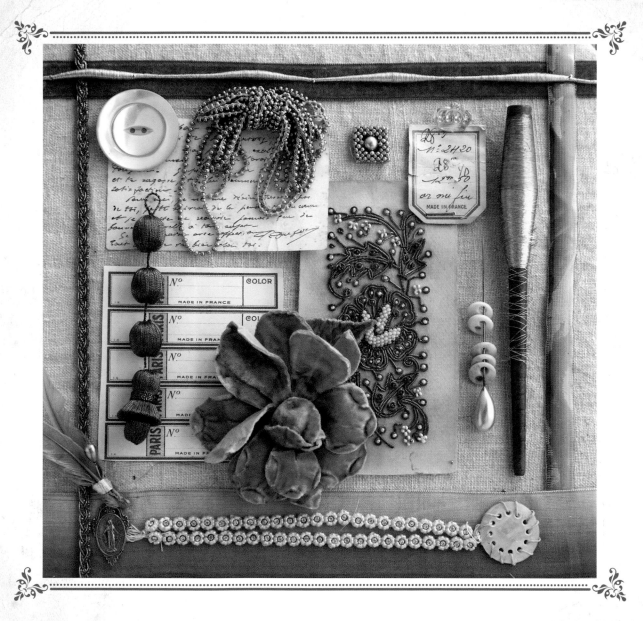

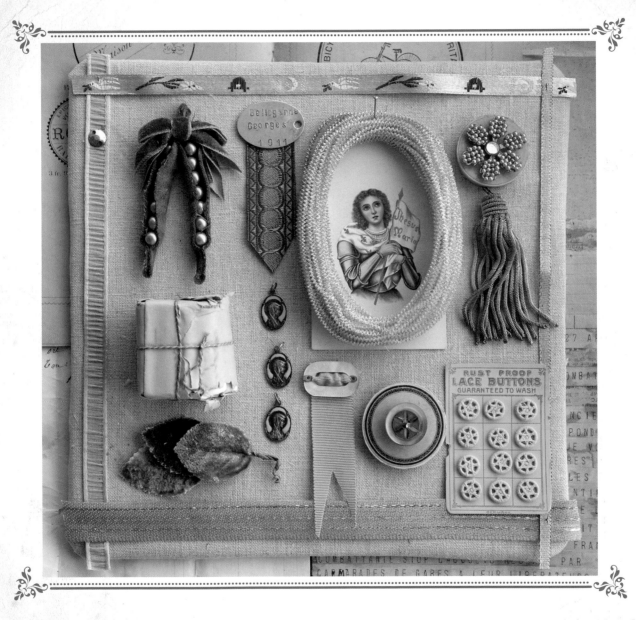

BUTTON CHARM BRACELET

Mother-of-pearl buttons, cabachons, glass beads

This simple bracelet uses all sorts of old mother-of-pearl buttons, embellished with *cabachons* to dress them up even more. *Cabachons* are gemstones with rounded tops and flat bottoms—ideal for affixing to flat surfaces. Use wayward buttons that have fallen off your favorite dresses, or pick up old button cards at the flea market. Flat buttons glued onto the bezels work best, although buttons with shanks will work too— just thread with a head pin and loop onto the chain. Continue adding buttons over the years and you will have an heirloom bracelet to pass on to your children.

❖ MATERIALS ❖

- ❖ Clasp
- ❖ Rosary pliers
- ❖ $7\frac{1}{2}$ in to $8\frac{1}{2}$ in/19 cm to 22 cm cable chain
- ❖ Jump rings (sixteen $\frac{1}{8}$ in/3 mm, two $\frac{3}{16}$ in/5 mm, and one $\frac{1}{3}$ in/8 mm)

- ❖ Glue (epoxy or jeweler's)
- ❖ About 16 old mother-of-pearl buttons in random sizes (I used $\frac{1}{2}$ in/11 mm, $\frac{5}{8}$ in/15 mm, and $\frac{3}{4}$ in/18 mm)
- ❖ Bezels with rings attached (random sizes to fit your buttons)

- ❖ *Cabachons* or small flat-back buttons (to embellish center of buttons)
- ❖ About 15 glass drops embedded with wire
- ❖ Cutting pliers

DIRECTIONS

1 Attach the clasp to the chain by opening a 3/16-in/5-mm jump ring with the rosary pliers and linking the end of the chain to the ring on the clasp. Close the jump ring. Attach a 1/3-in/8-mm jump ring onto the opposite end of the chain; this will give the clasp a large ring to link onto when closed.

2 Glue each of the buttons onto their respective bezels. Be sure that the bezel you choose covers the whole surface of the button, so that the glue will adhere and the button won't fall off. Let dry for at least an hour so the buttons set fully.

3 Once dry, glue decorative *cabachons* on top of the buttons for extra flair. You may also use small, flat-back glass buttons on top of the mother-of-pearl for a bit of sparkle. Let dry again.

4 Using 1/8-in/3-mm jump rings, open, and attach a button *cabachon* to the chain. Close the jump ring. Continue until all of the button *cabachons* are attached. Think about balance and weight—try to keep the weight even on the chain so the bracelet wears comfortably.

5 With cutting pliers, cut the wire of the glass drops to 1/2 in/12 mm, then make a loop with the rosary pliers, leaving a small gap to link it to the cable chain. Attach it to small links on the cable chain and close the wire with the rosary pliers. Continue attaching the glass drops.

LITTLE LADIES

BASEMENT TREASURES

Metallic ribbon, trim, and fabric

Years ago, my sister, Molly, and I were digging through the Porte de Vanves flea market in Paris and found the most delicate little dancer figurine. Handmade a century ago, she had a wire body, a delicate hand-painted face, and a tiny tutu stitched out of old organza. To Molly, it represented something old and tattered, yet beautiful and elegant. After some agonizing, she handed over all of her francs and brought the tiny dancer home. Inspired by those small details and whimsical charm, these statues could even be used as a cake topper for a very special occasion.

❧ MATERIALS (FOR ONE LADY) ❧

- Hot glue and hot glue gun
- Wooden bead (for head), about ½ in/12 mm
- Small wooden dowel or toothpick, about 2½ in/6 cm long
- X-ACTO knife
- Wire cutters

- 12½ in/32 cm millinery wire
- Pliers
- 1 roll white florist's tape
- Craft glue
- Cotton pearl embroidery floss (assorted colors for skin, hair, and shoes)

- Assorted scraps of metallic fabrics, ribbons, and trims
- 1 button or small piece of cord
- Acrylic paint for lips, eyes, and base
- 3 small paintbrushes
- 2-in/5-cm wooden disc
- Drill

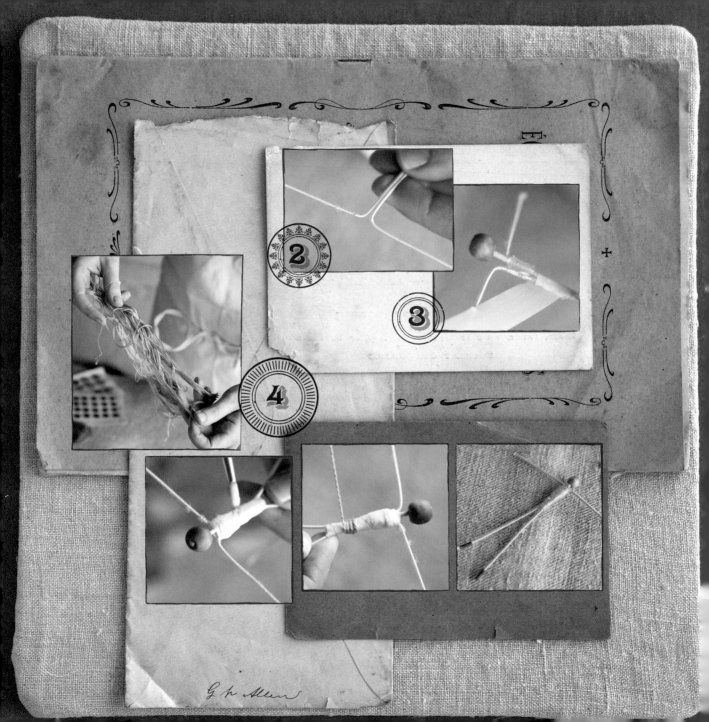

DIRECTIONS

1 Glue the wooden bead (head) onto one end of the dowel using the hot glue gun. When the glue has cooled, trim the dowel with an X-ACTO to about 1¼ in/3 cm.

2 Using wire cutters, cut the millinery wire into two 6¼-in/16-cm pieces. Bend each of the wires at a right angle with the pliers, 2 in/5 cm from one end. The 2-in/5-cm sections will be the arms. Center the dowel between the two pieces of wire, with the head placed a little bit above the "shoulders." Hot glue the wire pieces to the dowel. Allow the glue to cool.

3 Wrap florist's tape around the glued section, starting at the "waist." Continue wrapping around and around, using more tape in the torso of the doll to pad the area. Wrap until you have achieved the desired body shape.

4 Starting at the waist of the doll, paint a strip around the doll about ½ in/12 mm wide with craft glue and then wrap the glued area with embroidery floss. Working in small sections this way, continue to wrap the entire doll—body, neck, arms, and legs—with floss. Stop wrapping about ½ in/12 mm from the bottom of each leg. Cut the floss close to the doll and cover the end with glue to secure. Switch to a different floss color to make the shoes. On one leg, leave about ¼ in/6 mm unwrapped (this will be the leg that is attached to the base).

continued . . .

. . . *continued*

5 Once the doll is dry, experiment with making clothes out of the scraps of fabric and ribbons. Ribbon makes a great bodice, tiny braids can be straps, and fringe can make a flapper dress. Hot glue the clothing to your doll.

6 Using craft glue, attach hair to the doll's head. Twist more embroidery floss into curls or unravel it to make soft waves. Finish the outfit off with a hat or head-band made from a button or bit of cord.

7 Using paintbrushes and acrylic paint, add lips and eyes to your doll's face.

8 Paint the wooden disc (base). When the base is dry, drill a small hole slightly off-center. Do not drill all the way through the base.

9 Bend your doll's limbs into an attractive position. Fill the hole in the base with hot glue and push the unwrapped section of the one foot into the hole. When the glue has cooled, use an X-ACTO to remove any glue that spilled out of the hole.

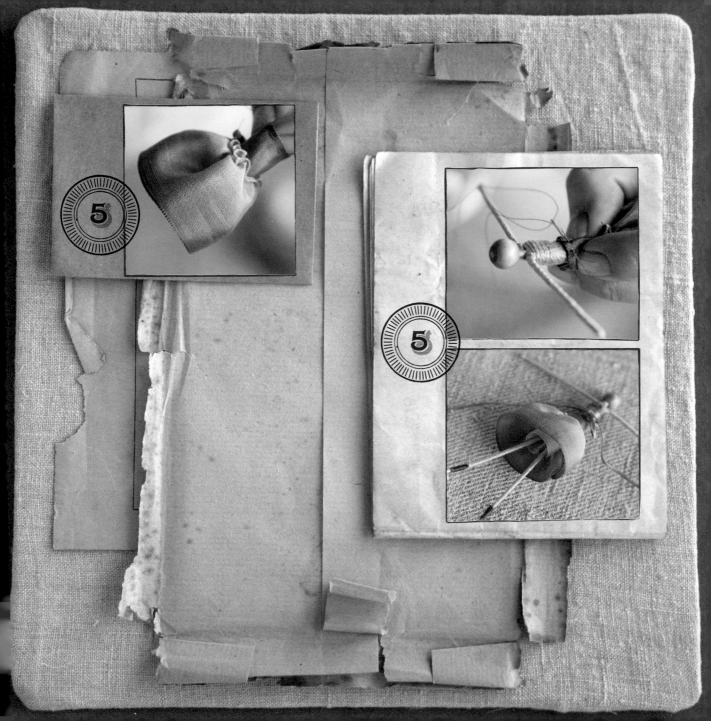

EMBROIDERED PINCUSHION

Metallic ribbon, old velvet material

Simple, elegant pincushions—treasures to any sewer—are rare these days. Making a beautiful pincushion takes some time, but it will hold pins forever. The simple floral design in this pincushion is inspired by a 19th-century pincushion I found in an antique shop in upstate New York. I was told the original embroidery stitch was called the "stitch of death" because so many women went blind mastering this stitch. Use the less-dangerous satin stitch to embroider the top of your cushion. The hidden gem of this cushion is on the inside: crushed walnut shells fill the cushion so it will sit firmly on your sewing table. I love it when function and beauty meet.

✧→ MATERIALS ←✧

- 9 by 12-in/23 cm by 30.5-cm piece off-white felt
- Embroidery marking pen
- Embroidery hoop
- Embroidery needle
- Embroidery floss, assorted colors
- Scissors
- 5 by 5-in/12 by 12-cm square velvet scrap
- ½ yd/0.5 m metallic ribbon, about 1½ in/4 cm wide
- Thread matching ribbon color
- Cotton batting
- Crushed walnut shells (found in pet supply stores)
- Funnel

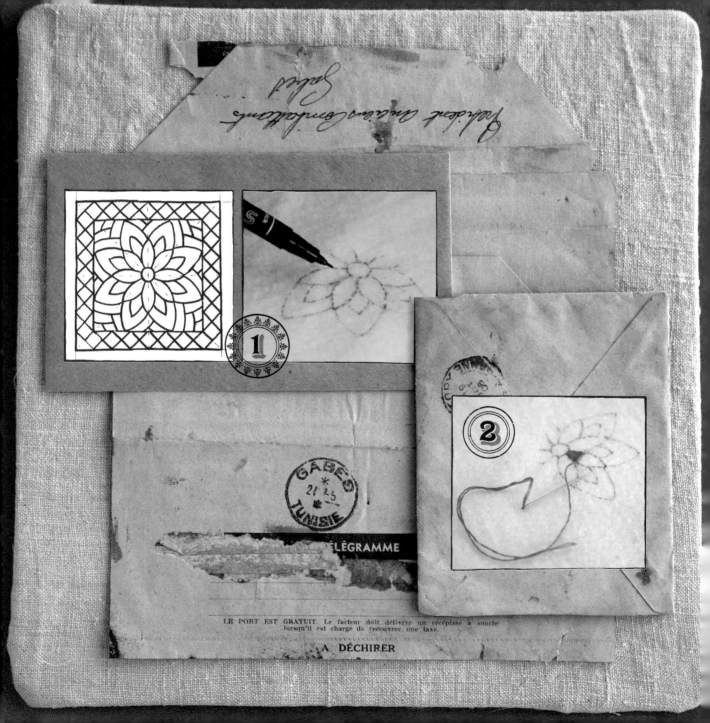

DIRECTIONS

1 Enlarge the design for the pincushion top provided on page 78 by 230 percent and then transfer onto the felt using an embroidery marking pen. Center the design in the embroidery hoop, making sure the design is still square before you begin to embroider.

2 Using the embroidery needle and floss, fill in all the areas of the design using a satin stitch. Vary the direction of the satin stitching to add interest. You may follow the photographs when choosing your colors, or fill areas in with whatever colors you wish. Make sure to completely cover the fabric so that no felt or pen markings are visible.

3 Once your pincushion top is embroidered, cut away excess $1/8$-in/3-mm seam allowance on all sides.

4 Cut a $4^1/4$-in/11-cm square from the velvet for the pincushion bottom.

5 Cut a $16^1/2$-in/42-cm piece of ribbon. With right sides together, sew the short ends of the ribbon with matching thread, creating a circle. Finger press the seam to one side.

continued . . .

. . . continued

6 With wrong sides together, hand sew one edge of the ribbon around the pincushion top with more matching thread, just inside the embroidered design. Sew the other edge of the ribbon to the pincushion bottom, leaving a 2-in/5-cm opening for filling.

7 With embroidery floss, cover the seam allowance with a satin stitch around all raw edges, but still leaving the 2-in/5-cm opening unfinished.

8 Fill your pincushion with a combination of cotton batting and, using a funnel, crushed walnut shells. Walnut shells give the pincushion some weight and they contain a natural oil that keeps your needles and pins sharp and conditioned.

9 Once filled, hand sew the opening closed and finish the satin stitching.

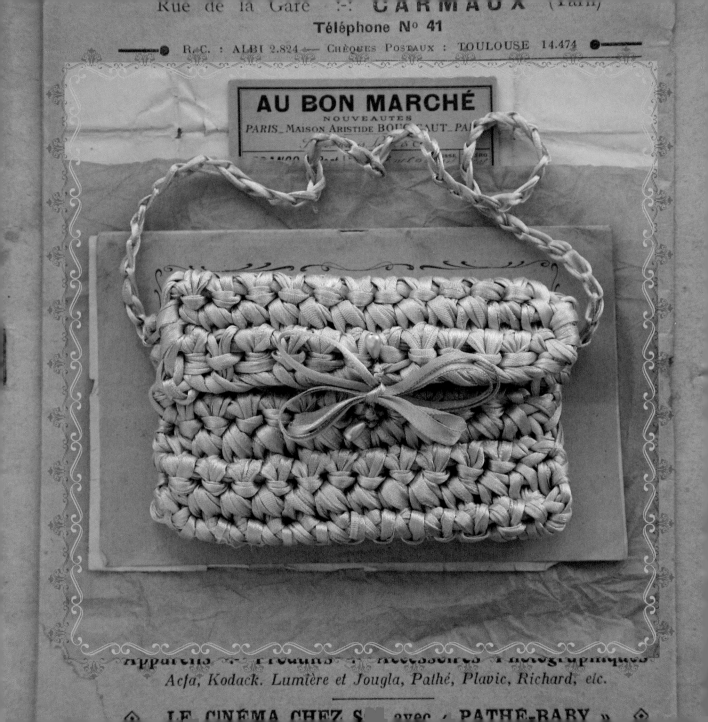

CROCHETED METALLIC PURSE

BASENT TREASURES

Metallic ribbons, beads

I'm always in search of the perfect bag—a little purse that will sparkle all on its own. The metallic ribbon in this design shimmers and shimmies all over, begging to be brought to a cocktail party. Over the years, the mesh ribbon softens, aging well and adding to the strength of the mesh. A metallic-colored yarn would also work well for this design. Finished off with a simple closure of thin silver ribbon and embellished with a pearl or two for luck, this is something to wear over your shoulder forever.

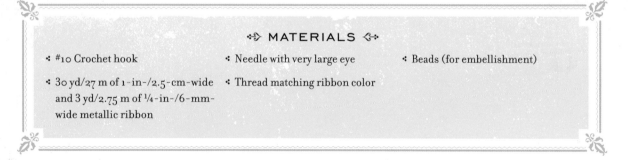

❖ MATERIALS ❖

- #10 Crochet hook
- 30 yd/27 m of 1-in-/2.5-cm-wide and 3 yd/2.75 m of ¼-in-/6-mm-wide metallic ribbon
- Needle with very large eye
- Thread matching ribbon color
- Beads (for embellishment)

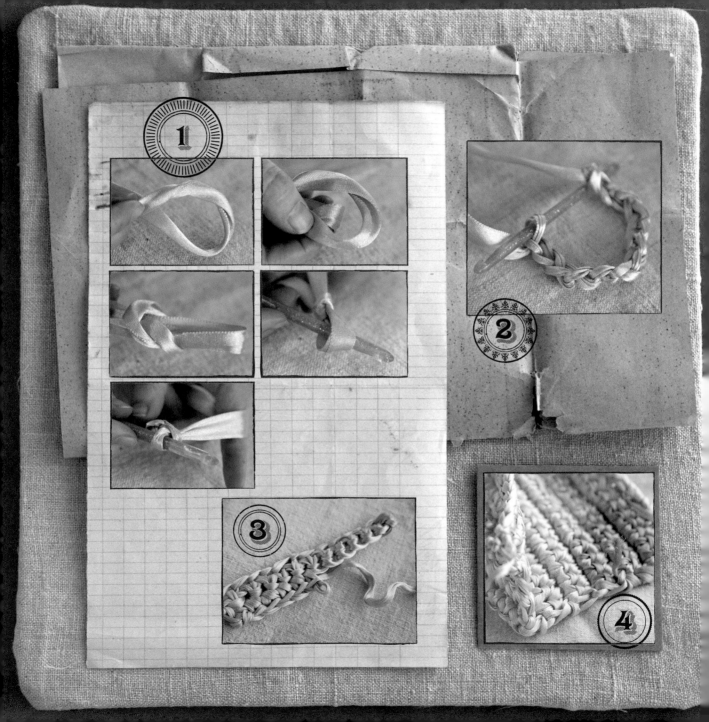

DIRECTIONS

1 Make a slipknot onto the crochet hook with the 1-in-/2.5-cm-wide ribbon, and begin a chain stitch.

2 After 14 single chain stitches (or enough to reach 8 in/20 cm), turn and double crochet 14 stitches.

3 Double crochet another 20 rows, or until the piece is 8 in/20 cm wide by 11 in/28 cm long.

4 Tie off securely and cut the ribbon, leaving about a 6-in/15-cm tail. Using the needle, weave this tail back inside the crochet to hide it and trim any excess. Fold the bottom of the bag two-thirds of the length up to create the pouch.

5 Thread your remaining ribbon on the needle. Sew the side of the clutch together with a diagonal whipstitch, going up in one direction and back in the other direction, creating a cross stitch for a decorative design. Cut and tie off your ribbon inside the clutch and repeat on the opposite side.

6 To make a shoulder strap, repeat step 2 with the ¼-in-/6-mm-wide ribbon. Make sure to leave about a 6-in/15-cm tail before your slipknot. Chain stitch until your strap is the desired length. My strap is 22 in/ 56 cm long.

7 Tie off the end of your chain stitch, thread the ribbon on the needle, and sew the handle inside the clutch.

continued . . .

. . . continued

8 To ensure your flap folds nicely, weave a line of ribbon in and out along the fold line. Once you have completed the row, cut the ribbon, leaving at least 6 in/15 cm of the tail and tie off. Weave any remainder tail into the clutch.

9 To make the tie closure, cut 14 in/ 35.5 cm of ¼-in/6-mm ribbon and thread both ends into the front bottom part of the clutch. Knot on both sides. Repeat for the top half of the clutch.

10 Using needle and thread or head pins, attach old pearls, beads, or buttons for embellishments.

IMPRIMERIES RÉUNIES S. A., LAUSANNE
Imprimé en Suisse

SPECIMEN SHADOWBOX

BASEMENT TREASURES

Beetle, old velvet material

When I found a box full of dried beetles in Tinsel Trading's basement, I knew I had to create a special case to display the beauty of their natural color, especially the green iris underbelly. This shadowbox is ideal for any precious collection. If you don't have access to a box full of beetles, or if bugs are not your idea of beauty, think about framing a natural element such as an egg, a pinecone, a seedpod, or even a small nest—something that is too pretty not to honor. Look for richly colored velvet and antique-looking papers, like the old page from a Deyrolle student sketchbook I used to decoupage the outside of the box.

❧ MATERIALS ☙

- Pencil
- Scissors
- Small screwdriver
- Plain wooden box with shadowbox lid (available in craft stores)
- Scientific illustrations or book pages

- Sponge brush
- Liquid patina
- Small paintbrush
- Mod Podge
- Acrylic paint
- White felt

- Craft glue
- Cotton velvet
- Hot glue and hot glue gun
- Beetle or other object to place under glass

DIRECTIONS

1 Unfasten the shadowbox portion of the box lid and set aside. Trace the base and sides of the box onto the paper to create a template. Cut out the template. Remove any hinges or latches from the box with a small screwdriver. To antique them, use the sponge brush to paint with liquid patina until the desired look is achieved. Set the hardware aside to fully dry.

2 Decoupage the exterior of the box with Mod Podge, paintbrush, and decorative paper you've chosen. Edges that are too small to be covered can be painted with coordinating acrylic paint. Build up layers of Mod Podge until you are happy with the box's finish.

continued ...

. . . continued

3 Cover the inside of the shadowbox backing with the white felt, using craft glue. Cover the other side with velvet. When the glue has dried, use the craft glue or hot glue gun to attach the insect to the felt side. Add a small label next to the insect if you wish.

4 Line the inside of the box with velvet, gluing in place with craft glue.

5 Reassemble the shadowbox with the hardware.

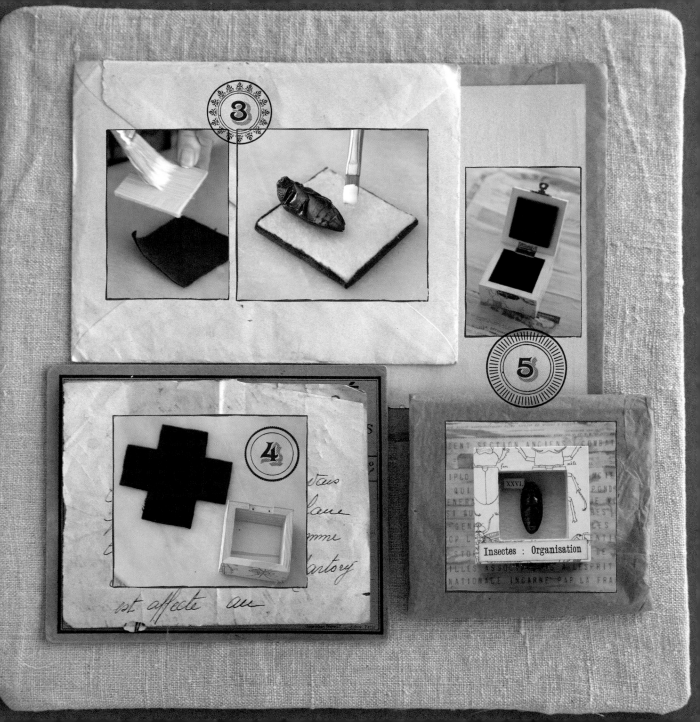

Insectes : Organisation

Plants - Plantes

Adresse Télégraphique :
TOURR

Tourrette-Fitère

Arbres - Fleurs Coupées

MAISON de CULTURE
SAINT-RÉMY - PROVENCE

JAPANESE TEMARI BALL

Metallic thread, tassel

A thousand-year-old craft from Japan, the *temari* ball was traditionally given as a wedding gift or present between good friends as a symbol of luck, promise, and love. This French interpretation of the classic ball is wrapped with yards and yards of metallic threads and some of my favorite embroidery threads. To make the ball into a decorative ornament, attach a tassel and a loop for hanging. Spend some time making this traditional craft as a wedding gift for an old friend.

❖➤ MATERIALS ➤❖

- 3-in/7.5-cm Styrofoam ball
- Yarn (approx. 30 yd/27 m)
- Cotton sewing thread matching yarn color
- Long embroidery needle

- Ball head pins
- ¼-in-/6-mm-wide strip of paper
- Scissors
- Gold and silver metallic thread

- Embroidery floss in assorted colors
- Measuring tape
- Large tassel

DIRECTIONS

1 Start by wrapping the ball with yarn. Wrap randomly but evenly, until none of the Styrofoam is visible underneath. Switch to the sewing thread, and wrap until no yarn is visible, then use the embroidery needle to stitch through the layers to hide the end of the thread.

2 Place a pin in the ball. This will be the "north pole." Determine the circumference of the ball with a paper strip by wrapping from the north pole around the ball and all the way back. Fold the paper strip back in half to determine half of the circumference. Place another pin at the "south pole."

3 Fold the strip of paper in half again, and use it to mark the "equator" of the ball, placing 4 pins along this line. Use the folded piece of paper to equally space the pins around the equator, ending with 6 pins that are all equidistant from each other.

4 Cut a piece of metallic thread, long enough to go around the ball four times (plus a little extra). Knot the thread at one end, and after threading on an embroidery needle, insert the needle about $\frac{1}{2}$ in/12 mm from one of the "poles." Bring the needle out at the pole, pulling the thread through until the knot is buried in the ball. With the metallic thread, divide the ball into eight segments, wrapping thread around the pins as you go. Take small stitches in the ball at the pins to keep the lines straight. Keep the pins in the ball.

continued . . .

. . . continued

5 Folding your paper in half again, divide each metallic thread guideline in half, and mark with pins.

6 With your first color of embroidery floss, thread the needle and knot at the end. Burying the knot in the ball as you did in step 4, bring the thread out at the north pole. You can now remove that pin. Stitch a square around the guide threads by taking small stitches under the guide and long diagonal stitches to the next guide thread. (If you have ever made a God's Eye, the process is very similar.) Make four or five rounds with the first color. Finish by taking the needle deep into the ball, bringing it out some distance away, and cutting the floss close to the ball.

7 Work the pattern in the same way with each new color, adding as many rounds of each color as you like. In between colors, use the metallic threads to add variety. Try to keep the work as square as possible, checking with a measuring tape occasionally. When you reach the pins you placed in step 5, that square is done.

8 Repeat steps 6 to 7 at each of the remaining 5 pins placed in step 3, for a total of 6 squares. You can make each square the same, or vary the pattern, so long as they are all the same finished size. When the squares are all completed, the corners of each square should touch.

9 Fill in the triangular spaces between squares with decorative stitches in gold thread.

10 Choose what points on the ball will be the top and bottom, and sew a tassel at the bottom and a loop at the top with gold thread. Hang your ball from the loop.

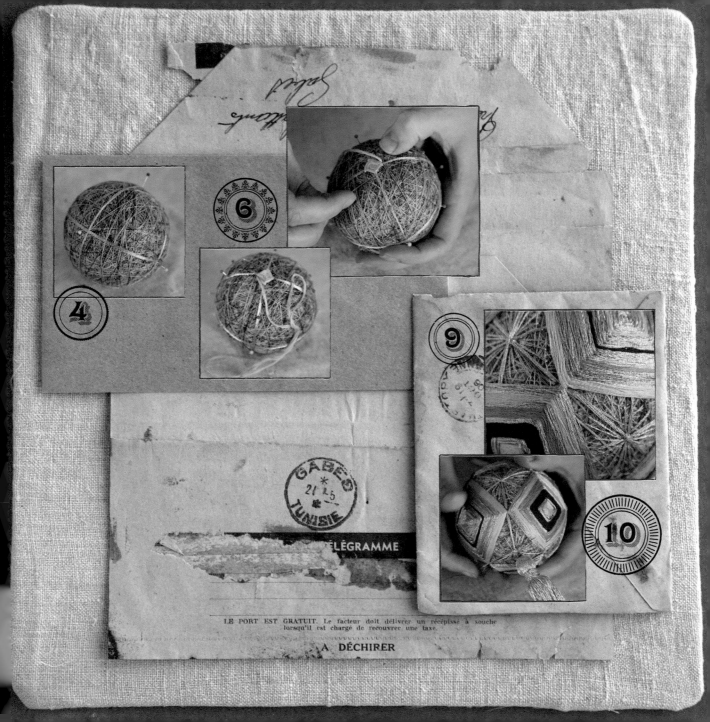

EGG SHRINE

Metallic sequins, trim, mica

I have always loved building small altars—whether it's for a special holiday or just to display a well-loved find. This egg was inspired by the highly detailed, decorative eggs Carl Fabergé made during the end of the 19th century. Made of precious metals, hard stones, and enamel, Fabergé's eggs were the ultimate luxury gift to the Czar. This version, made with a real goose egg and painted porcelain blue, is decorated with old metallic sequins. Inside, a thin layer of mica makes a glowing background for the *Virgen de Guadalupe*, who reigns inside the small shrine.

❧ MATERIALS ❧

- Blown goose egg
- Pencil
- Goggles
- Mask
- Dremel with a diamond disc cutting bit

- Sandpaper (120 grit)
- 2 small paintbrushes
- Acrylic paint
- Transparent iridescent paint
- About 50 sequins, rhinestones, or beads

- About 12 in/30.5 cm silver braid trim
- Clear drying adhesive cement (made for gluing metals, ceramics, or glass)
- Tweezers
- Styrofoam scrap for figure's base

- White glue
- Mica or glitter
- 1 cotton ball
- Small figurine
- Purchased stand

DIRECTIONS

NOTE: Breathing eggshell dust can be very harmful. Always wear goggles and a respirator mask when carving eggs, and work in a ventilated area.

1 Begin by marking your egg with pencil lines to determine the best position for the window. Draw the shape for the window, taking care to make it as symmetrical as possible.

2 Don the goggles and mask, and using the Dremel on a low speed, carefully cut the shell along the pencil line. Don't worry if the cut isn't perfectly smooth. When the entire window is cut out, lightly sand the opening until it has a smooth edge.

3 Paint the exterior of the egg with a small paintbrush and acrylic paint. When the color is dry, add a layer of iridescent paint using another paintbrush. Make sure the inside of the egg is clean of any dust and paint the inside with the iridescent paint as well.

4 Once the paint is completely dry, embellish the outside of the egg with sequins and braid. You may want to draw light pencil lines dividing the egg so that your placement of jewels is even. Glue the sequins and braid in place using adhesive cement and tweezers. Wear your mask and work in a ventilated area when working with the adhesive.

continued . . .

. . . continued

5 Cut a piece of Styrofoam that fills the bottom of the egg, making a platform for your figure. Glue it in place with the white glue.

6 Cover the inside of the egg with a layer of white glue and sprinkle mica over it. Shake off any excess. Pull apart a cotton ball to cover the Styrofoam base, leaving a small hole in the center of the base uncovered for your figure.

7 Using adhesive cement, glue the figure in place. Hold the figure in place with tweezers until it sets.

8 Display your egg on a purchased stand.

TASSEL NECKLACE

BASEMENT TREASURES

Buttons, beads, ribbon, coiled wire beads, tassel

Embellished with vintage buttons, beads, and ribbon, this necklace has lots of old-world charm. Inspired by a box full of tassels in all different shades of metallic—silver, bronze, gold, and copper—I designed this necklace to look and feel as if it had been worn by a flapper in the 1920s. The second strand is made up of old coiled wire beads threaded onto chain. This coiled wire was actually made on the machines in the Tinsel basement—a specialty of Tinsel Trading! Create the look with coiled wire beads and a tassel from your favorite craft or drapery store.

❖❯ MATERIALS ❬❖

- Clasp
- 2 cable chains (one about 20 in/ 50 cm and one about 18 in/46 cm)
- 4 jump rings (three ³⁄₁₆ in/5 mm and one ¹⁄₃ in/8 mm)
- Rosary pliers
- Tapestry needle

- 22 in/56 cm of ¼-in/6-mm silk ribbon
- Needle
- Thread matching the ribbon color
- Two 7-mm buttons
- 2-in/5-cm tassel

- Scissors
- Twelve ¹⁄₃-in/8-mm beads and thirty-four ¹⁄₆-in/4-mm glass beads
- Forty-eight 1-in/2.5-cm head pins
- Cutting pliers
- 21 coiled wire beads

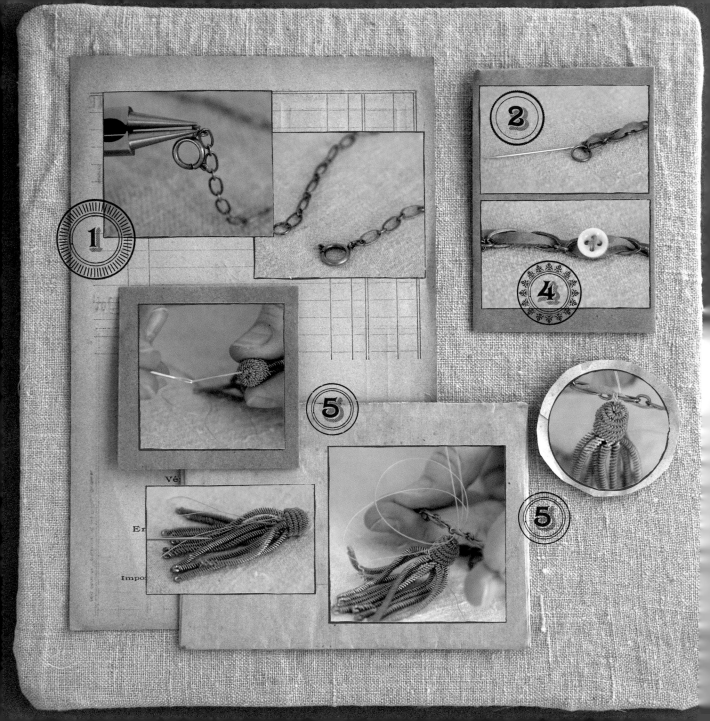

DIRECTIONS

1 Attach the clasp to the longer chain by opening a $^3/_{16}$-in/5-mm jump ring with rosary pliers and linking the end of the chain to the ring on the clasp. Close the jump ring. Attach a $^1/_3$-in/8-mm jump ring onto the opposite end of the chain; this will give the clasp a large ring to link onto when closed.

2 Thread a tapestry needle with the silk ribbon and begin weaving the ribbon in and out of the cable chain.

3 Once you have sewn the length of the chain, stitch each end closed using the needle and thread. You can wrap the ribbon around the chain once or twice and then stitch down through the cable of the chain; this will keep the ribbon in place on the chain.

4 Sew the buttons onto the ribbon. If you make sure your clasp is always to the left, both buttons will face forward when you wear the necklace.

5 Find the center of the necklace and sew on the tassel. With a threaded needle, come up through the bottom of the tassel, and sew through the chain link a few times. Be sure to go through the cable and the ribbon to secure well. Stitch down through the top of the tassel and pull the thread down the length of the tassel, hold with a finger, and thread the needle back up through the bottom of the tassel. Cut the thread to make a fringe. Repeat this step to add more fringe.

continued . . .

. . . continued

6 Thread a glass bead onto a head pin and cut the wire down to ½ in/12 mm with cutting pliers. Make a loop with the rosary pliers; do not close the loop. Attach to the chain, then completely close the wire. Continue attaching glass beads up both sides of the necklace, alternating between small and large beads.

7 Thread coiled wire beads onto the second, shorter piece of chain and attach to the back of the tassel necklace with ³⁄₁₆-in/5-mm jump rings; this will make up your second strand.

LUCKY HORSESHOE

Metallic sequins, glass hearts, mother-of-pearl buttons

I like to imagine that back in the day people who traveled with the circus or carnival had to make portable amulets and good luck charms to ward off evil spirits. Hung in their caravans, they were the women's handiwork. This velvet horseshoe is covered with old sequins, mother-of-pearl buttons, and bits and pieces collected from many basement digs. The metallic and grayish teal color palette gives the horseshoe the age and patina of a well-traveled amulet. Hang your horseshoe over the entrance to a room so all who enter will be blessed with a bit of luck.

❖❯ MATERIALS ❮❖

- Pencil
- Paper (about 8 ½ in by 11 in/21.5 cm by 28 cm)
- Pins
- Scissors
- ¼ yd/23 cm gray velvet

- ¼ yd/23 cm canvas or cotton twill (optional)
- Needle
- Thread
- Assorted old sequins, buttons, and beads
- Fabric glue (optional)

- Wire hanger
- Wire cutters
- Masking tape (optional)
- Batting (about 2 large handfuls)
- 1 yd/1 m gold braid
- 2 yd/1.8 m ribbon

DIRECTIONS

1 With the pencil, draw a horseshoe shape on the paper about 7 in/17 cm tall and 6 ½ in/16.5 cm across at the widest point. Add ¼ in/6 mm all the way around the shape for a seam allowance. Cut out your pattern.

2 Pin the pattern to the velvet. Cut two horseshoe pieces out of the velvet. If your velvet is very thin or floppy, back it with a sturdier fabric by stitching the backing fabric to the wrong side of the velvet, just inside the seam allowance.

3 Hand sew sequins and beads onto one horseshoe piece. Stop attaching the sequins about ½ in/12 mm from all the edges of your piece to make turning easier. Hand sewing the embellishments adds a true vintage look, but, to save time, you can adhere them using fabric glue made specifically for attaching sequins and rhinestones.

4 Pin right sides together and sew horseshoe pieces together, leaving a 4-in/10-cm opening at the bottom edge. Trim the corners and clip the seam allowance around the curves. Turn right side out and press with your fingers.

continued . . .

. . . continued

 5 Bend and cut the hanger wire with wire cutters to fit inside the horseshoe. This will keep the shape from collapsing. Cover the wire ends with masking tape if they are too sharp. Fill the horseshoe with batting until it is firmly stuffed. Sew the opening closed.

6 Cover the entire seamed edges with gold braid, either by hand sewing or gluing. Sew two 1-yd/1-m ribbons to the top points of the horseshoe and tie in a bow for hanging.

PETITE PRIZE MEDALS

BASEMENT TREASURES

Metallic and grosgrain ribbon, beaded appliqués

Award a friend on a landmark birthday, for a grand achievement, or just because she or he holds a special place in your heart. These small prize ribbons are made with many of the materials that were once used to make military medals of honor. Old metallic ribbon with a sequined and beaded appliqué sewn on top makes up medals fit for a king. If you can't find any old appliqués, try using *ombre* ribbon to make small rosettes.

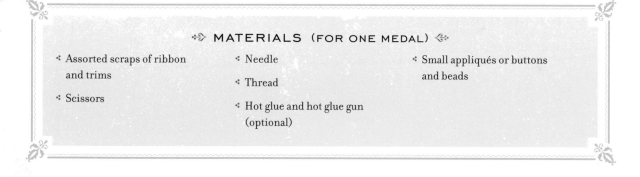

❖ MATERIALS (FOR ONE MEDAL) ❖

- Assorted scraps of ribbon and trims
- Scissors

- Needle
- Thread
- Hot glue and hot glue gun (optional)

- Small appliqués or buttons and beads

DIRECTIONS

1 Cut a piece of ribbon 3 in/7.5 cm to 5 in/12 cm long. At one end, fold the ribbon in half and trim at a diagonal, creating a double point.

2 At the other end of the ribbon, fold twice on the wrong side to hide the raw edge. Sew or glue the folded edge.

3 On the right side of the ribbon, sew or glue small pieces of trim or braid across the top edge, folding the raw edges of the braid under so they won't unravel.

4 Sew or glue appliqués or buttons and beads onto the ribbon.

5 Hand sew the finished medals to a bag or piece of clothing, display them in a shadowbox frame, or attach a safety pin and wear as a brooch.

MILLINERY FLOWER PIN

BASEMENT TREASURES

Metallic fabric and ribbons, stamens

Metallic fabric can be very heavy—the metal threads weigh down the fabric. A wedding dress during the 1920s may have been made using metallic fabric and would have weighed over 10 pounds/4.5 kilograms! For a small decorative embellishment using the same fabric, fashion a rose with metallic fabric petals. Sew a small pin on the back and you have a corsage that won't wear you down and will stay fresh forever.

❖ MATERIALS ❖

- Paper
- Pencil
- Pins
- Scissors
- Assorted scraps of metallic fabrics
- Needle
- Thread
- 9 flower stamens
- Hot glue and hot glue gun
- 6 in/15 cm medium-weight wire
- Felt scrap
- White florist's tape
- Pin back (available at craft or bead stores)
- 12 in/30.5 cm ribbon

DIRECTIONS

1 On a piece of paper, draw three sizes of flower patterns, one about 6 in/15 cm in diameter, one 5 in/12 cm, and one 4 in/10 cm. Each flower should have four petals of equal size.

2 Pinning your patterns to the fabric, cut out two flowers of each size from various metallic fabrics. Stack the flowers, with the smallest on the top and each layer slightly rotated so the petals are not even with one another. Secure the stack together by hand sewing with needle and thread through the center with a few small stitches.

3 Sew a loose gathering stitch in a circle around the center of the stack of flowers, and pull tight until the flower puckers in the middle. Secure the gathering with a few tight stitches and knot off.

continued . . .

. . . continued

4 Fold your stamens in half and secure them to the center of the flower with small stitches from the back of the flower through all the layers. Add a drop of hot glue if you feel they are not secure enough.

5 Bend your piece of wire in half, and poke both ends through all layers of the flower, so that the bend in the wire covers the center of the flower stamens. (You may need to poke a starter hole for the wire using a small, sharp pair of scissors.) Twist the wires together at the back of the flower.

6 Cover the back of the flower with a small circle of felt about 1¼ in/3 cm in circumference, with a hole in the center for the wires to poke through. Hot glue the felt in place. Next, wrap the wires with florist's tape to cover them. Attach the pin back to the covered wire with more florist's tape.

7 Hot glue the ribbon to the back of the flower for more embellishment. If your flower is too floppy, use small drops of hot glue between petals to give it more structure.

SEQUINED BIRD

BASEMENT TREASURES

Sequins, feathers, glass glitter

This little feathered friend brings a bit of the garden inside. Covered with old silk chenille, sequins, and feathers, this bird is set to sing a song. You can either thread a loop onto the top of the bird and hang it as an ornament or fasten a small clip onto the bottom of the bird and clip it onto a perch. If you don't have old chenille on hand, use ribbon or even wool yarn to cover the bird's body. Try hand curling the feathers for the tail by running a blunt object along the spine of the feather, just like curling ribbon.

❧ MATERIALS ❧

- Craft glue
- One 1½-in-/4-cm- and one 1-in-/2.5-cm-diameter Styrofoam balls
- Small paintbrush
- White chenille
- Gold glitter

- Straight pins
- Sequins
- Scissors
- Brown felt or heavy paper scrap
- Straight pins with black heads or small black beads (for eyes)

- Feathers
- Hot glue and hot glue gun
- Sawtooth clip (available in craft stores)

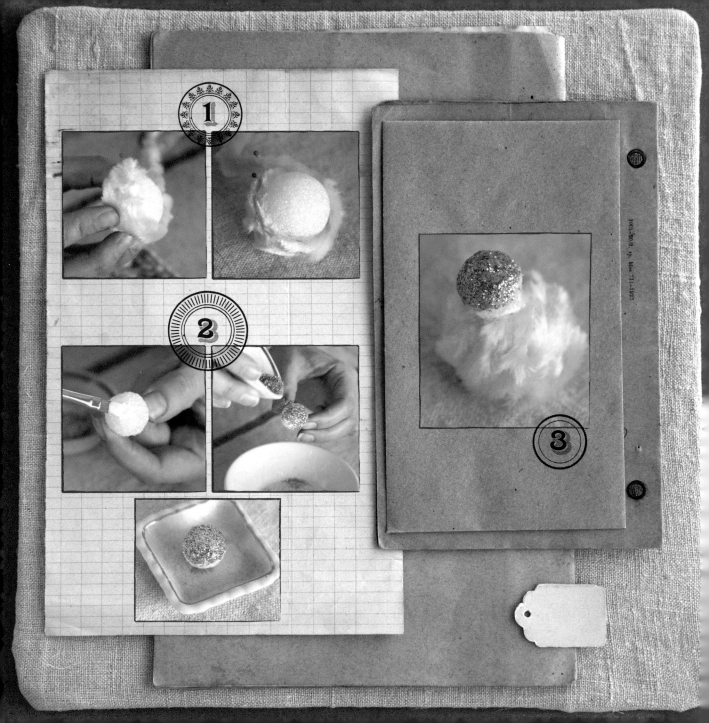

DIRECTIONS

1 Spread glue on the larger Styrofoam ball (the body) with the paintbrush and wrap the chenille around the circumference. Leave one end of the ball with a small uncovered spot for inserting the tail feathers.

2 Spread glue on half of the smaller ball (the head), and sprinkle with gold glitter to cover.

3 Once both balls are completely dry, glue the head to the body, keeping in mind that the glittered part will be the face of the bird. Use straight pins to hold the head in place while it dries.

continued . . .

. . . continued

4 Cover the rest of the bird's head with sequins, using glue and straight pins to secure the sequins in place. Cut a small diamond shape for the beak from the brown felt and fold it in half. Glue it to the bird's face. Add black-headed straight pins for the eyes.

5 Glue feathers to the sides of the body for wings, and glue feathers for the tail in the uncovered spot at the end of the body. Add detail to the wings and tail with glitter and sequins.

6 Hot glue a clip to the underside of the bird's body and display by clipping the bird to a stand or tree branch.

OPERA BAG

BASEMENT TREASURES

Beads, old velvet material, tassel

Inspired by an antique opera binocular bag I found in Paris, this small bag is sewn out of old rose velvet and embellished with beads and a tassel. This petite bag will hold just the essentials. Look for an old tattered purse that has seen better days and gently cut off the frame to reuse with your new design. If you can't find an old frame, look for a frame at a sewing store that stocks unusual notions. The result: a small work of art that's as pretty to hang on the wall as it is to wear on your wrist.

❧ MATERIALS ❧

- Metal purse frame (should have holes along the edge for attaching fabric)
- Pencil
- Pattern paper (about 8 ½ in by 11 in/21.5 cm by 28 cm)

- Scissors
- ¼ yd/23 cm velvet
- ¼ yd/23 cm lining fabric
- Embroidery transferring pen
- Beading needle

- Thread matching the velvet
- Bugle beads
- Hand sewing needle
- Tassel

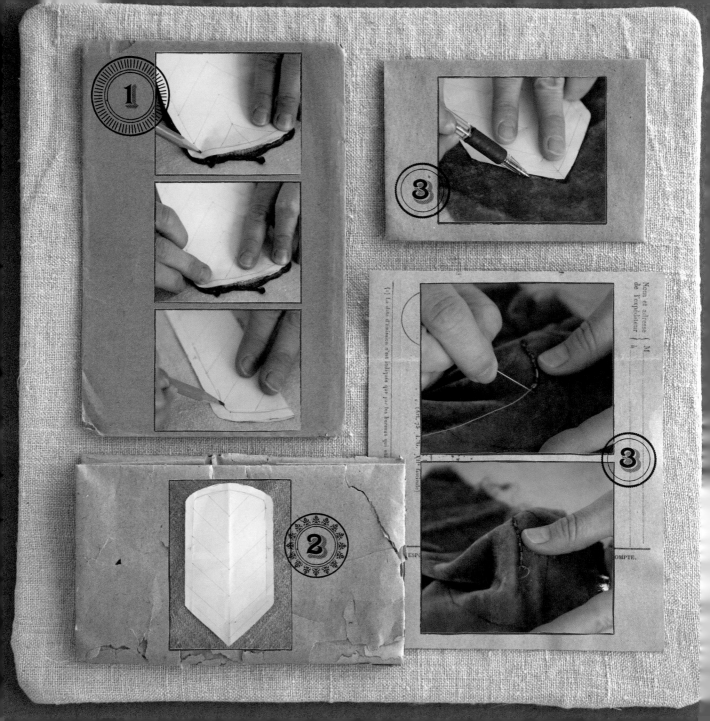

DIRECTIONS

1 Start by tracing the inside edge of your purse frame onto the pattern paper. This is the top of your purse pattern. Draw the sides of the purse by extending down from the corners of the frame, and draw the purse bottom 4 in/10 cm to 5 in/12 cm from the frame corners.

TIP: Fold the pattern along the center and only draw one side to ensure the pieces are symmetrical.

2 Add a ¼-in/6-mm seam allowance to all sides of the pattern. Draw a design for the beading on the pattern, making sure to keep the design from getting too close to your seam allowance. Cut two of the pattern pieces out of the velvet and two out of the lining fabric.

3 On one of the velvet pieces, transfer the beading design using the embroidery pen. Use a beading needle and matching thread to fill in the design with bugle beads.

continued . . .

. . . continued

 Sew the two velvet pieces, right sides together, at the bottom and sides using a ¼-in/6-mm seam allowance. Trim corners, turn right side out, and finger press. Sew the lining together in the same fashion.

5 Put the lining inside the purse and slip stitch in place around the top edge, enclosing the seam allowance of both layers. Sew the purse to the holes in the frame using a whipstitch, with the thread doubled for extra strength.

6 Finish the purse by sewing a tassel to the bottom.

MEMORY BOOK

Metallic wire, old velvet material

Remember past friends and family with a small memento that can be kept close by. This miniature *recuerdo*, or memory, book houses a collection of photos. Find a small book with blank pages—an autograph book, a photo album, or a diary would work— and cover it with beautiful fabric. I used washed silk velvet. Once you have sewn a small cover for the book, use metallic beads or beads on wire to embellish the cover. Stitched carefully, this book will become a small heirloom worthy of being passed on.

❧ MATERIALS ☙

- Small journal with blank pages
- Pattern paper
- Pencil
- Pins
- Scissors

- Piece of velvet large enough to cover your book
- Measuring tape
- Matching cotton fabric
- Tailor's chalk
- Needle

- Thread (to match cord or braid)
- Thread (to match velvet)
- Metallic cord (about 2 yd/1.8 m)

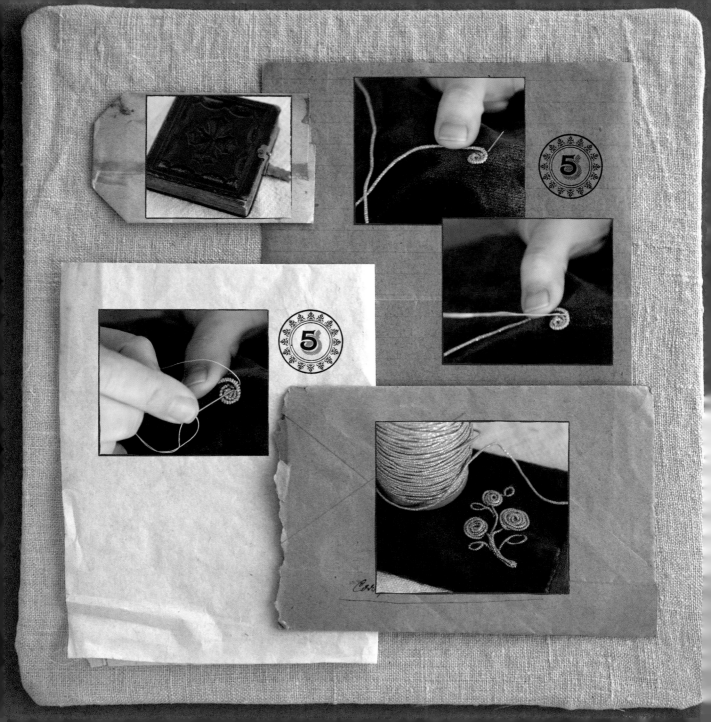

DIRECTIONS

1 Start by opening your book flat on the pattern paper and tracing the entire cover. If your book does not flatten all the way, measure the front and back covers and the spine, then draw a rectangle that corresponds to the total length measured. This is your cover piece.

2 Add ¼ in/6 mm to all sides of the cover piece. Pin the pattern to the velvet and cut it out.

3 Measure the inside covers of your book, and draw a rectangle on the pattern paper for the inside flap. Add ¼ in/ 6 mm to each side of the flap. Pin the pattern to the cotton fabric and cut out two pieces.

4 In the center of the right half of the cover piece, draw a small flower with the tailor's chalk. Keep it simple! If you find the chalk is too impermanent on velvet, sew basting stitches in a contrasting thread along the chalk line and then brush away the chalk.

5 Hand stitch the cord or braid along the design, with your stitches casting over the braid rather than through it. Keep any stitching at least ½ in/12 mm from the outside edges of the cover piece.

continued . . .

. . . continued

 Match the short ends of the cover piece with the corresponding side of the flap pieces. With wrong sides together, hand sew using a ¼-in/6-mm seam allowance.

7 Finger press the seam allowance toward the flaps. Turn the other raw edge of the flaps in ¼ in/6 mm and topstitch.

8 Finger press both long edges of the entire cover ¼ in/6mm toward the wrong side. Fold the flaps in toward the center, wrong sides together. Top-stitch around the entire cover, about ⅛ in/3 mm from the finished edge.

9 Slide the book inside the cover flaps.

NOTE: If your book has hardware, as ours did, you may need to cut slits for the hardware to fit through. Finish these openings by covering the edges with a tight satin stitch.

L'OISEAU BLEU

WIRED NEST AND EGGS

BASEMENT TREASURES

Gold metallic wire, colored wire

Finding an abandoned nest intact only happens a few times in one's life, so I was inspired to create my own out of old gold metallic wire. Add some small scraps to emulate a bird's material gathering and you'll have a soft resting spot for small wire-wrapped eggs or something sacred, like a handmade piece of jewelry or tiny love note.

❖ MATERIALS ❖

NEST
- Wire cutter or pliers
- 150 ft/46 m wound wire
- Scraps (stamens, leaves, buttons, other odd bits of old scraps)

ONE EGG
- Wrapping tissue paper or newspaper (about 5 in by 5 in/ 12 cm by 12 cm)
- Scissors

- Metallic thread or fine ribbon (about 7 yd/6.5 m)
- White glue
- Small pin

DIRECTIONS

FOR THE NEST

1 Cut the wound wire into fifteen 10-ft/3-m pieces.

2 Secure five pieces of wire together into a long length by twisting together at the ends. Wrap each group of five strands of wire the same way.

3 Start wrapping one of the groups of wire into a 1-in/2.5-cm circle and continue wrapping the wire around the circle to form a base for the nest.

4 Once you have your shape in place, wrap one wire around the others as you go—this will hold the shape. Thread the wire in and out to secure the shape of the nest. Continue wrapping this first bundle of wire together to secure the bottom layer of the nest.

5 Wrap the other two bundles of wire onto the nest the same way, taking time to stop and secure the shape of the nest by shaping it together with your hands. This step is quite unstructured—think of a nest and try to imagine the layers that go into building one.

6 Weave the scraps into the nest either by tying them to the wire with a scrap of wire or wrapping them around the wire—think of these as the embellishments of the nest.

continued . . .

. . . continued

FOR ONE EGG

7 Using your hands, form a small egg shape out of the tissue paper or newspaper. Tissue paper is softer and tends to mold easier.

8 Cut a 20-ft/6-m piece of metallic thread or ribbon and wrap it around the egg until you can no longer see the paper. Take your time wrapping the egg—you want to cover it from side to side and end to end.

9 Glue down the end of the thread using a small pin or needle to hold it in place while drying.

RESOURCES

Although most of the supplies used for the crafts in this book are available from Tinsel Trading in New York, you may also want to visit some of these small gems that carry all sorts of vintage notions and materials. Many sell their materials online as well.

SHOPS

ACCESSORIES OF OLD

This huge collection of embellishments and vintage fashion accessories comes from the largest South African haberdashery of the 1920s.

4822 St. Elmo Avenue, Bethesda, MD 20814
(301) 760-7228
www.accessoriesofold.com

BERGER BEADS

The oldest and largest supplier of new and vintage beads and findings in Los Angeles, Berger Beads has been family owned since 1941. There is something for everyone at Berger!

413 E. 8th Street, Los Angeles, CA 90014
(213) 627-8783
www.bergerbeads.net

D. BLUMCHEN

"Purveyors of Life's Little Niceties" is how D. Blumchen explains itself—and it truly is! This wonderful site is filled with antique tinsel and metallic Dresden foil trims.

www.blumchen.com

LA DROGUERIE

A fun boutique with multiple locations around France that stocks all sorts of craft supplies, including beads, buttons, fabric, and yarn.

9-11 Rue du Jour, 75001 Paris, France
www.ladroguerie.com

JENNIFER OSNER

Jennifer offers antique textiles as well as boxes and boxes full of old notions and bits from the 19th and 20th centuries. A great source for quantity, Jennifer buys out huge old lots of goods.

www.jenniferosner.com

MOLINE

Filled with new and old passementerie and textiles, this is a great source of inspiration next time you find yourself in Paris. The tassels alone are worth the trip.

1 Place Saint-Pierre, 75018 Paris, France
www.tissus-moline.com

NIFTY THRIFTY DRY GOODS

This wonderful collection of goods is about "the admirable in domestic useable art, the proven beauty of vintage 'exquisitry,' and the grace of traditional notions." Susan Gower presents her vintage beauties in collections of color alongside her handmade pincushions.

www.niftythriftydrygoods.com

ROSE MILLE

This collection of old notions started with a large milliner's lot bought by the owner, Michelle Rose Jorgensen. You'll find vintage and more at this Stillwater, Minnesota, shop.

125 South Main Street, Stillwater, MN 55082
(651) 439-0205
www.rosemille.com

SCRAP

SCRAP stands for Scroungers' Center for Reusable Art Parts and it is a warehouse filled with treasures. Donations come from all sorts of manufacturers—textile printers, frame shops, jewelry makers, and science labs, just to name a few. This is a great place to find recycled materials on a budget.

801 Toland Street, San Francisco, CA 94124
(415) 647-1746
www.scrap-sf.org

SHINE GALLERY

I like this site for a bit of the odd and unusual. Shine sells old store stock—all sorts of vintage memorabilia including old bakelite dice and chalkware carnival prizes. If you are not looking for something in particular, you might find exactly what you need!

www.shinegallery.com

TAIL OF THE YAK

Look for old trinkets and magical treasures in this gem of a shop full of wonder and inspiration.

2632 Ashby Avenue, Berkeley, CA 94705
(510) 841-9891

THEATRE OF DREAMS

Only open six times a year for special events, this is a magical place filled with Wendy Addison's art and imagination.

11 Canyon Lake Drive, Port Costa, CA 94569
(510) 787-2164
www.wendyaddison.net

TINSEL TRADING Company

The original source of inspiration for this book, Tinsel Trading will offer you a wonderland of old and new materials for crafting and inspiration.

1 West 37th Street, New York, NY 10018
(212) 730-1030
www.tinseltrading.com

VINTAGE FASHION

Visit Beth and Julie Guernsey, a mother-daughter team, online or at one of the many vintage textile shows where they exhibit their treasures. They collect and present the crème de la crème.

www.1860-1960.com

VINTAGE PASSEMENTERIE

A wonderful, small selection of French millinery ribbon, metallic trim, and *passementerie* buttons. Limited but elegant stock from the 1920s and '30s.

8600 SE Stark Street, Portland, OR 97216
(503) 256-8600
www.vintagepassementerie.com

VV ROULEAUX

One of my favorite shops in London filled with thousands of ribbons, trimmings, tie-backs, and flowers—even online, it's full of inspiration and color.

Cliveden Place, London, SW1W 8AX
020 7730 3125
www.vvrouleaux.com

Flea Markets

Flea markets are one of the best places to hunt and gather one-of-a-kind notions and fabrics. Build a collection over time and you'll always have a special scrap on hand to make something exquisite.

ANTIQUES BY THE BAY (CA)

Held the first Sunday of every month in Alameda, California, this market is always packed. More than 750 dealers sell wonderful old collectibles and vintage craft materials.

www.antiquesbythebay.com

BRIMFIELD ANTIQUE AND FLEA MARKET (MA)

Located in Brimfield, Massachusetts, this huge flea market is held three times per year. Plan to spend at least 2 or 3 days walking through the fields hunting down treasures.

www.brimfield.com

PASADENA CITY COLLEGE FLEA MARKET (CA)

A small, curated flea market held the first Sunday of every month. I like this market for the small collections brought out by local dealers. There's always a good bargain to be found at PCC!

www.pasadena.edu/fleamarket

PORTE DE VANVES (PARIS)

One of my very favorite Paris markets, just a short metro ride south from the center of Paris. Every Saturday and Sunday, look for old notions, textiles, and found objects at this classic French flea market.

www.pucesdeparis-portedevanves.com

STURBRIDGE ANTIQUE TEXTILE & VINTAGE FASHION SHOW (MA)

This indoor textile and notion show runs for one day during the Brimfield Market week. You'll find plenty of vintage dealers selling everything from sewing notions to beaded bags.

www.vintagefashionandtextileshow.com

ACKNOWLEDGMENTS

Thank you, Marcia, for finally letting me explore your basement—I hope this book is a small tribute to the collection of materials that your grandfather began and what you continue to collect and display at Tinsel Trading. Molly, I couldn't have done the deep dig without you—thank you!

Jody, thanks for taking my simple ideas and crafting them into something beautiful. As always, I feel very lucky to work with such amazing talent. Thanks also to Maggie and John, who both jumped in at the eleventh hour, lending their creative hands.

To my family, especially my mom and dad, thank you for keeping me balanced.

Jon, thank you for the beautiful photographs and the vision you bring to our projects . . .

Last, but not least, thank you to Kate, our editor, who believed we would uncover old notions and make something beautiful.

INDEX

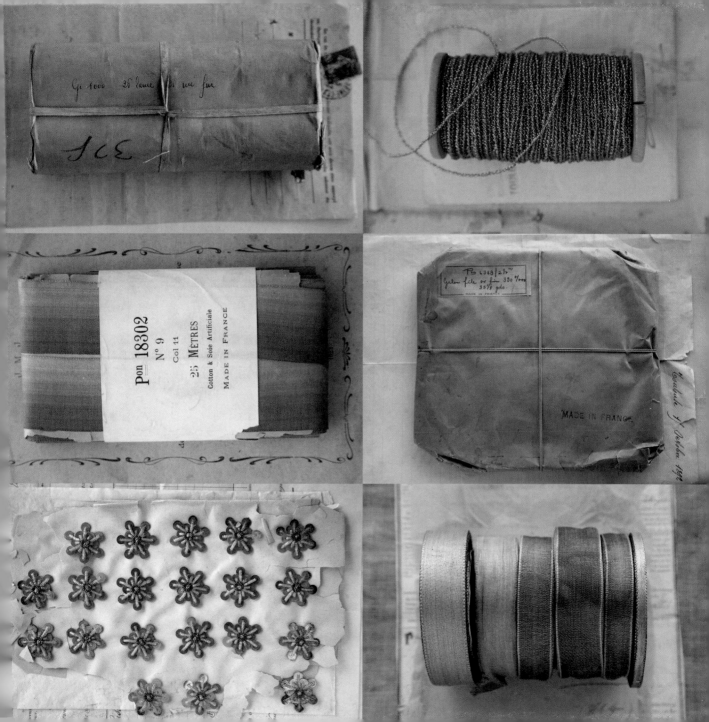